This book is dedicated to all my students enrolled in my day care center over the past several years. They have been my inspiration in writing poetry.

I want to express my appreciation to Jim Bodiford for his encouragement in writing this book.

I also want to thank Rebecca Morris for all her wonderful illustrations.

To order additional copies of this book, contact:
Xlibris
1-888-795-4274
www.Xlibris.com
Orders@Xlibris.com

ISBN:	Softcover	978-1-4134-3757-7
	EBook	978-1-4771-6497-6

Print information available on the last page

Rev. date: 02/06/2020

TABLE OF CONTENTS

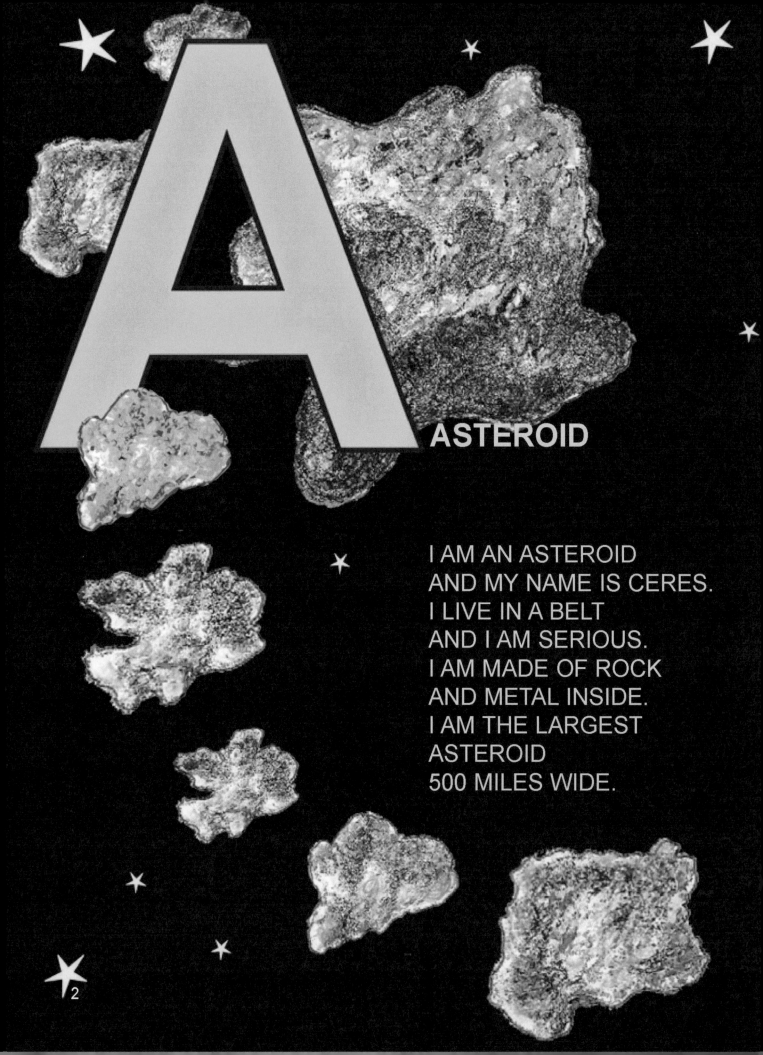

A

ASTEROID

I AM AN ASTEROID
AND MY NAME IS CERES.
I LIVE IN A BELT
AND I AM SERIOUS.
I AM MADE OF ROCK
AND METAL INSIDE.
I AM THE LARGEST
ASTEROID
500 MILES WIDE.

B

BRAIN

MY BRAIN IS AN IMPORTANT
PART OF ME.
IT MOVES ALL MY PARTS
AS YOU CAN SEE.
IT MAKES ME THINK
SO I CAN TELL
YOU ALL THE THINGS
I KNOW SO WELL.

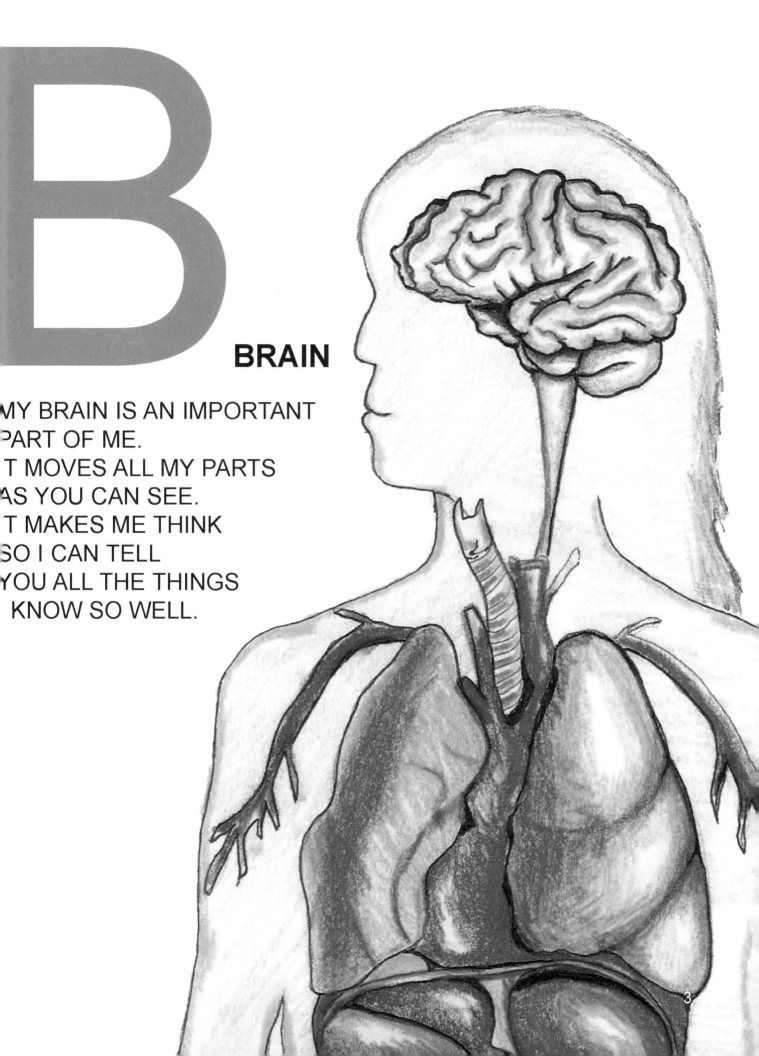

C

CHLOROPHYLL

CHLOROPHYLL IS MY NAME.
I AM GREEN AND ON A LEAF.
IN THE AUTUMN I FADE AWAY
AND THE COLORS ARE
UNDERNEATH.

D
DEW

THE GRASS IS WET
DO YOU KNOW WHY?
THE WATER IN THE AIR
FALLS DOWN FROM THE SKY.
WHILE WE ARE SLEEPING
IT FALLS DOWN TO
THE GROUND
WHEN WE WAKE UP
WE WILL HAVE DEW
ALL AROUND.

E

EARTH

THE EARTH ORBITS AROUND THE SUN
THAT MAKES OUR 4 SEASONS.
IT MOVES CLOSE AND FAR AWAY
THAT IS THE REASON.
THEIR NAMES ARE VERY SPECIAL
AND I KNOW THEM ALL.
WOULD YOU LIKE TO HEAR THEM?
WINTER, SPRING, SUMMER AND FALL.

F

FULCRUM

A BLOCK OF WOOD CAN
BE A FULCRUM.
IT CAN MAKE A LEVER.
ONE SIDE GOES UP AND
ONE SIDE GOES DOWN.
NOW THAT IS REALLY CLEVER.

GASES

THERE ARE THREE GASES
WE ARE TOLD.
FREON KEEPS THINGS
NICE AND COLD.
HELIUM TOOK MY
BALLOON UP IN A TREE.
IT IS A GAS THAT WE
CANNOT SEE.
OXYGEN IS A GAS
THAT WE SHARE.
WE ALL BREATHE
IT FROM THE AIR.

HIBERNATION

WHEN IT IS VERY COLD
AND SNOW IS ON THE GROUND
WE DON'T SEE A LOT
OF ANIMALS RUNNING AROUND.
THEY SLEEP ALL WINTER
WHICH MAY BE LONG
SO WHEN THEY WAKE UP
THEY WILL BE STRONG.

9

ICE

WHEN WATER IS A LIQUID
THE MOLECULES MOVE AROUND.
WHEN THE WATER IS 32 DEGREES
THE MOLECULES WILL
SLOW DOWN.
WHEN THEY FINALLY STOP
TOGETHER THEY WILL LOCK
FORMING A SOLID -
UPON IT YOU CAN KNOCK.

JUPITER

I AM THE 5TH PLANET
YOU CAN SEE ME IN THE SKY.
USUALLY I AM THE
BRIGHTEST THAT IS THE
REASON WHY.
I HAVE A RING LIKE SATURN
BUT IT IS NOT QUITE THE SAME.
IT IS MUCH SMALLER
AND JUPITER IS MY NAME.

K

KATYDID

THIS IS AN INSECT
THAT LOOKS LIKE A LEAF
TO KEEP IT SAFE FROM
ANIMALS, OH GOOD GRIEF!
IT IS IN THE
GRASSHOPPER FAMILY
BUT IT IS NOT
QUITE THE SAME.
IT IS GREEN AND
LIVES IN A TREE
AND KATYDID
IS IT'S NAME.

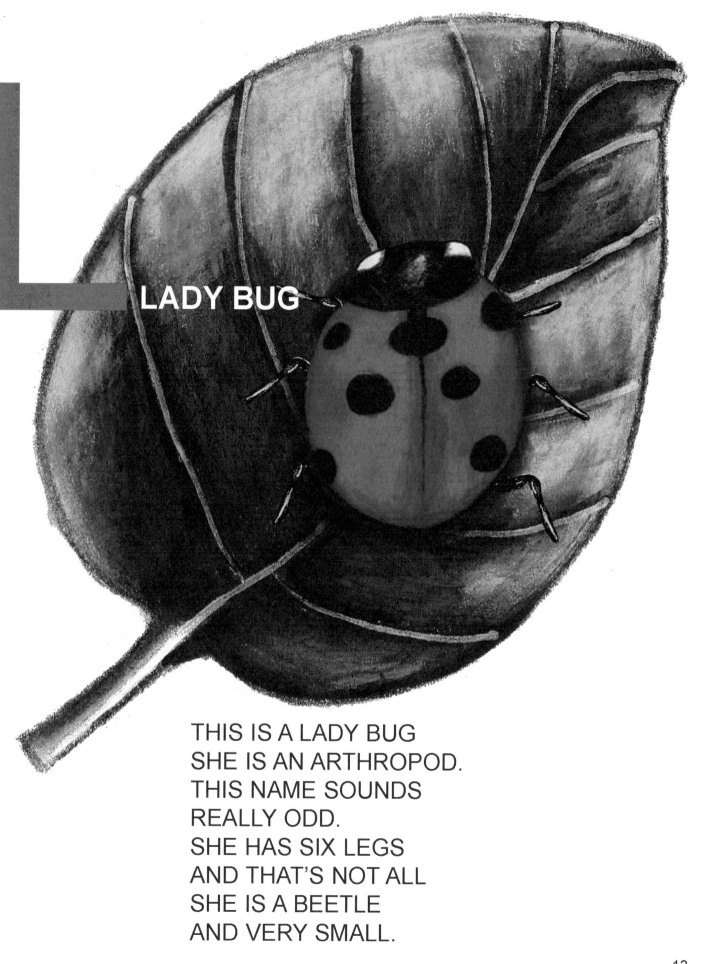

LADY BUG

THIS IS A LADY BUG
SHE IS AN ARTHROPOD.
THIS NAME SOUNDS
REALLY ODD.
SHE HAS SIX LEGS
AND THAT'S NOT ALL
SHE IS A BEETLE
AND VERY SMALL.

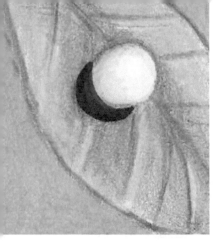

M
METAMORPHOSIS

METAMORPHOSIS IS A WORD
THAT MAKES THINGS CHANGE
LIKE TADPOLES AND
CATERPILLARS -
THEY EVEN CHANGE
THEIR NAME!

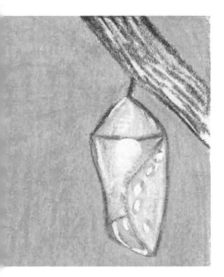

14

N

NERVOUS SYSTEM

A NERVOUS SYSTEM
IS IN ANIMALS
AND HUMAN BEINGS TOO.
IT TELLS OUR BODY
EXACTLY WHAT TO DO.
T INCLUDES OUR SPINAL CORD,
OUR NERVES AND OUR BRAIN.
IF WE DIDN'T HAVE IT, WE
WOULD NEVER BE THE SAME.

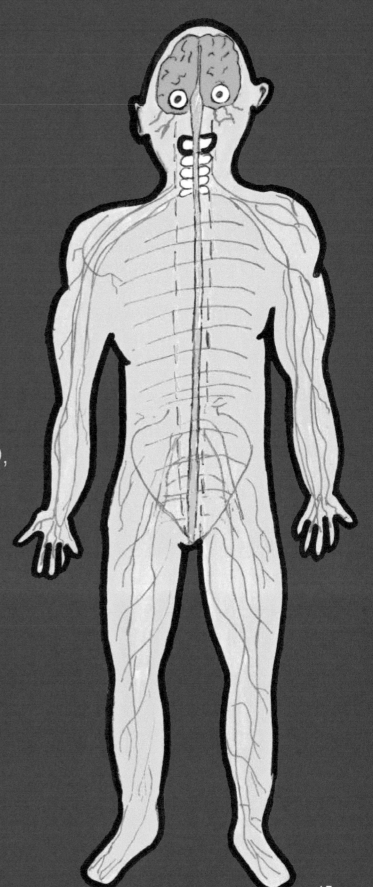

O

OCTOPUS

AN OCTOPUS IS A SEA ANIMAL.
HIS EIGHT ARMS ARE VERY LONG.
IF ONE BREAKS OFF
HE GROWS ANOTHER BACK ON.
HE HAS LARGE EYES
AND HIS BODY IS ROUND.
IN THE BOTTOM OF THE OCEAN
HE CAN BE FOUND.
HE HAS THREE HEARTS
ISN'T THAT STRANGE?
EVEN HIS COLORS
HE CAN CHANGE.
HE HAS NO BONES
AND THAT'S NOT ALL,
HE CAN BE BIG
OR HE CAN BE SMALL.

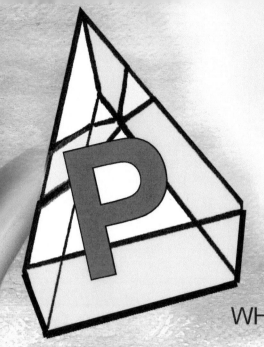

PRISM

WHAT IS A PRISM?

IT IS AN ODD SHAPED PIECE OF GLASS.
WHEN THE LIGHT SHINES THROUGH IT
IT WILL BEND AS IT DOES PASS .
LIGHT DOES THE SAME WITH RAINDROPS
THEY ACT LIKE PRISMS TOO.
IT IS INTERESTING TO SEE
EXACTLY WHAT THEY CAN DO.
SO NOW YOU KNOW THE MAGIC
OF MANY COLORS ALL AGLOW
THE NEXT TIME IT RAINS
WHEN YOU SEE THAT
BEAUTIFUL RAINBOW.

Q

QUOKKA

I AM A QUOKKA
I WILL TELL YOU
WHAT I DO.
I LOOK LIKE A
SMALL KANGAROO.
IT IS HOT IN
AUSTRALIA.
AS A RULE,
I LICK MY FEET, TAIL
AND BELLY SO
I CAN KEEP COOL.

R

RED-BACK SPIDER

I AM A RED-BACK SPIDER
AND THAT IS A FACT.
I AM BLACK WITH A RED
STRIPE DOWN MY BACK.
I LIVE IN AUSTRALIA
DID YOU KNOW THAT KIDDO?
I AM ALSO RELATED TO
THE BLACK WIDOW.
I AM DANGEROUS AS
YOU WILL SEE.
BE SURE THAT YOU
NEVER PLAY WITH ME.

S

SHOOTING STAR

A METEOROID IS A LUMP OF ROCK
THAT IS CALLED A SHOOTING STAR.
IT TRAVELS THROUGH
THE ATMOSPHERE
AND GOES VERY FAR.
IT IS VERY, VERY HOT AND
IT BURNS IN THE SKY,
LEAVING A TRAIL OF
BRIGHT LIGHT
WAY UP HIGH.

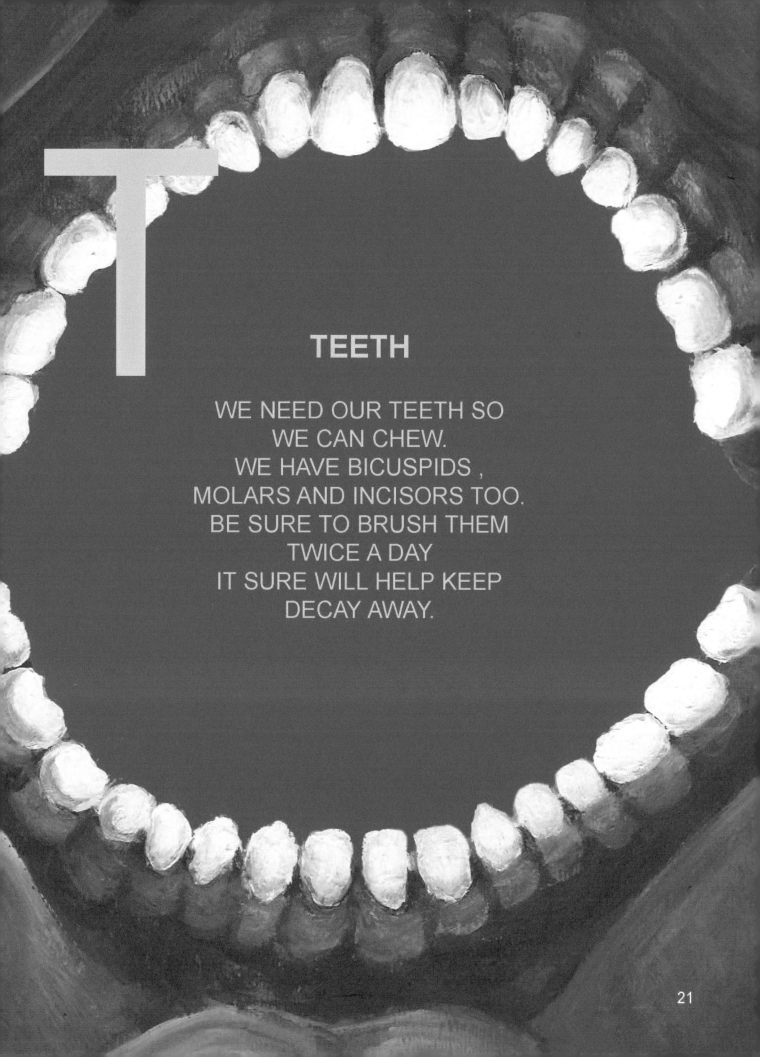

T

TEETH

WE NEED OUR TEETH SO
WE CAN CHEW.
WE HAVE BICUSPIDS ,
MOLARS AND INCISORS TOO.
BE SURE TO BRUSH THEM
TWICE A DAY
IT SURE WILL HELP KEEP
DECAY AWAY.

U

UNIVERSE

THE UNIVERSE IS MADE UP OF
EVERYTHING IN SPACE.
THERE ARE PLANETS,
METEORS, COMETS -
IT IS QUITE A SHOWPLACE!
THERE ARE GALAXIES AND STARS
AND EVEN DUST UP THERE.
IF YOU USE A TELESCOPE YOU
MAY SEE THEM EVERYWHERE.

VENUS

I AM ONE OF THE PLANETS AND MY
NAME IS VENUS.
IF YOU LEARN ALL ABOUT US
YOU WILL BE A GENIUS.
DID YOU KNOW I AM
THE SECOND PLANET FROM THE SUN
BE SURE TO REMEMBER TO TELL
EVERYONE.

W

WATER

GUESS WHAT I FOUND OUT
THAT I DIDN'T KNOW?
THAT ANOTHER NAME
FOR WATER IS H2O.
"H" IS FOR HYDROGEN
WHICH MAKES TWO PARTS.
"O" IS FOR OXYGEN.
DON'T YOU THINK I'M SMART?
"O" IS IN THE MIDDLE,
TOGETHER THEY LOOK COOL,
CREATING A GREAT BIG MOLECULE.

X
XENON

XENON IS A GAS THAT YOU
CAN NOT TASTE.
THERE IS NO ODOR, NO COLOR
YOU MAY THINK IT IS A WASTE.
BUT IT IS AN IMPORTANT GAS.
I AM SURE I AM RIGHT.
WE USE IT IN SPECIAL LAMPS
SO THEY WILL LIGHT.

Y

YAK

HELLO MY NAME IS YAK.
I AM A WILD OX AND I AM BLACK.
I AM 1100 POUNDS AND SOMETIMES MORE
I CAN BE MEAN AND THAT'S FOR SURE.
MY FRIEND IS A GRUNTING YAK
AND SHE IS PRETTY TAME.
YOU CAN SEE THAT WE ARE
NOT QUITE THE SAME.
SHE IS MUCH SMALLER AND
HER FUR IS ALL WHITE.
EVEN SO, I THINK
SHE IS ALRIGHT.
SHE GIVES MILK AND
HAS A BUSHY TAIL.
IN TIBET, SHE CARRIES PEOPLE
AND EVEN THE MAIL.

ZOOLOGIST

I AM A ZOOLOGIST.
I WILL TELL YOU WHAT I DO.
I LOVE TO STUDY ANIMALS
AND TAKE CARE OF THEM TOO.
I STUDY HOW THEY LIVE
AND I WORK IN A ZOO.
I GIVE THEM LOTS OF LOVE
AS I AM SURE YOU DO TOO.

27

My inspiration comes from the children in my day care. Building self-esteem is extremely important for all children, especially young children. Stimulating their young minds is essential for their academic growth. Children continue to enjoy challenges as they grow. I believe poetry is an effective tool for helping children to memorize at a very young age.

I write poetry because it is the easiest way for children to remember concepts. I tried teaching the same concepts without poetry and found it to be less interesting and the concepts were soon forgotten.

After I wrote my first poem, the children followed the pattern. They memorized it quickly and felt proud of their accomplishment. This inspired me to continue writing.

Teaching is a very rewarding experience for me. It is exciting to see them learn concepts, internalize the information and relate it appropriately. This tells me that they actually understand what you are teaching them.

I love writing and teaching and will continue to do so as long as God allows.

Look for more titles in the Aunt Linda's children's books series to be available soon. For more information, please visit the website at www.auntlindasdaycare.com

Printed in the United States
By Bookmasters